Our Glorious Lord

F. B. Meyer

D1613263

Christian Focus Publications

© 1994 Christian Focus Publications Ltd.
ISBN 1-85792-103-8

Published by
Christian Focus Publications Ltd
Geanies House, Fearn, Ross-shire,
IV20 1TW, Scotland, Great Britain

Printed and bound in Great Britain by
Cox & Wyman Ltd, Reading, Berkshire

Cover design by Donna MacLeod

Contents

Chapter 1

The Hidings of God

'Verily thou art a God that hidest thyself, O God of Israel, the Saviour'
(Isaiah 45:15)

'Thou art a God that hidest Thyself,' the prophet Isaiah said, as he looked up from his study of the processes by which God was educating his people for their great destiny. Permitted an insight into the ways of God's providence, he had beheld the rise and fall of dynasty and empire, the captivity, the exile, the restoration, the gradual elimination of idolatry and impurity, and the fusing of the entire nation into a condition in which God could use it for his own purpose; and now breaking away from his long and intent scrutiny of the ways of God, he breaks out with the cry, 'Verily thou art a God that hidest Thyself, O God of Israel, the Saviour'.

It is an exclamation that often rises to our lips *in nature*. We are always treading in the recent footprints of God; entering chambers that he seems just to have left; catching the glow of light which has just fallen from his face; but we always miss him. We go forward, and he is not there, and backward, but cannot perceive him; we speak, and feel that he hears, but there is no reply; we look up, and know that he is looking down, but we cannot see him; we feel after him, and are conscious that his hand is somewhere within reach, but we never touch it.

Men talk of law, and force, but what are these expressions save confessions that God, the mighty worker, is hidden from our view?

What thoughtful man can look upon *the state of the world* without acknowledging, on the one hand, that God must be present, and yet feeling, on the other, that he is certainly concealed. He does not step out of the unseen to arrest the progress of crime and high-handed wrong. There is no sign of his displeasure. Though his name is constantly taken in vain he utters no word of remonstrance. Though his glory is constantly trodden under foot he does not strive nor cry. Though his help is invoked, the heavens do not rend, or the cherub wings become the chariot of his descent, as of old, to the Psalmist's thought. He cannot be far away; he evidently hears and observes and feels all, but who would dare to speak or act as bad men do unless men were wont to calculate upon God's concealment of himself?

In our own life also we have to do with the hidings of God. Some days we walk in the dark, unable to see his face or to feel him near; we sit in our deserted chambers; we puzzle over our insoluble problems; we ask our myriad questions. It seems then as though a thick veil hangs between us and him whom we love. We are not sensible of any sin or inconsistency which has caused him to withdraw, and yet there are the hidings of his face. Why has he taken that wife, or husband, or friend from our warm embrace, when so many another life, if similarly bereaved, would have felt it less? Why this passion for love without its satisfaction? Why this hunger for knowledge and service without gratification? From all these questions we turn, heartsick and weary, as Noah's dove from winging her flight over the restless water. We are conscious that the miracle of the gradual healing of the blind man is a parable of our experience. Our vision is but indistinct; we see men as trees walking. It will be necessary that the hand of Christ be laid again upon us ere we see all things clearly.

And yet we cannot wonder at the mystery which veils God and his ways. We are but children. Yesterday we were in the cradle; today we are sitting on the low form of the infant school. We have not yet commenced to graduate in the higher classes, and the faculties of the wisest and best amongst us, compared with those of the youngest angel, will probably range as those of a babe, when compared with the furthest acquirements of philosophic thought.

Besides, God has to graduate his revelation. Many mysteries have been unfolded to mankind in the later pages of the Bible, which were hidden from ages and generations. The sudden blaze of uncreated glory would dazzle, blind, and kill us. We could not bear the unveiled view of God. He must needs hide his glory as he passes by, revealing only his back parts. The revelation of the majesty of our Saviour was attempered to the ability of the disciples to bear it. The dawn of revelation, like that of the natural day, must be by almost insensible degrees.

And then, further, it is obvious that there are reasons for God's dealings with ourselves and with others, which he cannot disclose. If he did we should not understand. How often does a parent tell a child to wait, because there are things which cannot be explained; terms, the full meaning of which cannot be understood; relations, connections with others that involve principles which lie altogether beyond the range of immature thought. God has explained as much as our human faculties can apprehend, but there is much beyond our range; we see but part of his ways, and the thunder of his power we cannot understand. What if evil is stronger than we think? What if mere Omnipotence be powerless to deal with it, and that it can only be quelled by moral and spiritual processes? What if the moral benefit of the universe can be best promoted by allowing evil slowly to work itself out? What if the redemptive purpose needs time to assert its supremacy? What if the position of all beings and all worlds is being affected by the incidents which are transpiring upon the surface of our earth? We know so little. We stand upon the rim of inexplicable mysteries; our circle of light only reveals the surrounding realm of darkness.

Moreover, God must teach us to walk by faith and not by sight; what we see we cannot hope for. Where there are no rocks we need no pilot; where the path is plain we need no guide. It often happens that God says to his child, 'I must shadow from you the sensible enjoyment of my Presence; I must withdraw the sunlight from your path; I must lead you from the green pastures and still waters into the darkened valley; I must deprive you of emotion, for you will grow better in the dark; but trust me'. When, God hides from us so much that we would fain know, let us believe that the same love conceals, as at other times reveals, and that shadow and sun are accomplishing our growth in grace, and in the knowledge and love of God.

One consideration, however, is growingly precious - God is love. He that hides himself is also the Saviour. There is no question as to the essential nature of him who is working all things after the purpose of his own will. We know what friendship is. We can trust some souls so utterly that no act of theirs, however strange it seemed, could shake our faith in their unutterable love. Instead of interpreting their heart by an isolated act, we explain the act by the tender heart behind it. We dare to believe that whatever appears to militate against love is only another way of expressing it more deeply. Thus as we think of God and know him to be love, we stand in the sunshine of certainty, and everything settles into harmony and peace.

All attests his love. The adaptation of light to the eye, of sound to the ear, of love to the heart. Take out of human life sin and its consequences, and the residuum proclaims the beneficence of the Creator. We can account for the presence and power of much which is dark and forbidding, and for the rest we can trust. The love of kindred hearts; the rhythm and beauty of Nature; the evident purpose which is leading all events and minds to a goal of glory; above all, the revelation given to us through holy men, through the Son and by the Cross - all prove to us that God is a Saviour. All his purposes emanate from his heart; all his dealings have salvation as their end; all events beneath his strong hand subserve the aims of his redeeming grace. He is saving us; he is saving the world; he is saving the universe; the Saviour God is ever going forth upon his ministries of love, and whatever may daunt and bewilder is somehow consistent with a love so divine, so all-embracing, so infinite, that when the end has arrived the universe will be compelled to admit that not one act was inconsistent with its loftiest conceptions of divine tenderness.

Chapter 2

Suffered to Hunger

'All the commandments which I command thee this day shall ye observe to do, that ye may live, and multiply, and go in and possess the land which the Lord sware unto your fathers.

And thou shalt remember all the way which the Lord thy God led thee these forty years in the wilderness, to humble thee, and to prove thee, to know what was in thine heart, whether thou wouldest keep his commandments, or no.

And he humbled thee, and suffered thee to hunger, and fed thee with manna, which thou knewest not, neither did thy fathers know; that he might make thee know that man doth *not live by bread only, but by every word that proceedeth out of the mouth of the Lord doth man live.*

Thy raiment waxed not old upon thee, neither did thy foot swell, these forty years.

Thou shalt also consider in thine heart, that, as a man chasteneth his son, so the Lord thy God chasteneth thee. Therefore thou shalt keep the commandments of the Lord thy God, to walk in his ways, and to fear him.

For the Lord thy God bringeth thee into a good land, a land of brooks of water, of fountains and depths that spring out of valleys and hills;

A land of wheat, and barley, and vines, and fig trees, and pomegranates; a land of oil olive, and honey;

A land wherein thou shalt eat bread without scarceness, thou shalt not lack any thing in it; a land whose stones are iron, and out of whose hills thou mayest dig brass.

When thou hast eaten and art full, then thou shalt bless the Lord thy God for the good land which he hath given thee' (Deuteronomy 8:1-10).

From the foot of Pisgah Moses reviewed the wanderings of the forty years, and bade the people remember all the way by which they had been led. He recognised the leading of Jehovah in every step and every day of that terrible march, and with the clear-sightedness which comes at the end of an accomplished purpose, he saw something of God's meaning in it all. There were, apparently, three reasons why God chose the way of the wilderness as the route for Canaan, instead of the comparatively easy one along the shores of the Mediterranean.

The first purpose was that God

might humble his people. Theirs had been a wonderful history. For them the land of Egypt had been smitten with the ten plagues. For them the firstborn of Pharaoh had been stricken on the steps of the throne. For them ten thousand lambs had shed their life-blood on the eve of the Exodus. For them the Red Sea had cleft its waves, whilst Pharaoh and his host sank like a stone in its depths. For them angels had spread the daily breakfast on the desert sands. For them the rocks had flowed with water, and God himself had descended in a chariot of cloud. There was every danger, therefore, that the pride of their heart should rise, and lead them to think that there was something in themselves which had secured so great a succession of marvels. Therefore, God led them by the way of the wilderness, that, as they came face to face with its difficulties, they might be able to realise their impotence and dependence on himself.

This is a clue to the mystery of your life. This is why God permits you to come up against blank walls, to measure yourself in vain against immeasurable and infinite forces, to stand looking down into depths you cannot fathom, and up into heights you cannot reach - to peer in vain into the mists that roll around the edge of your little life. Thus you shall know yourself to be but finite, insignificant - a worm and no man - less than nothing, and vanity.

But there was a second reason why God led the people through the wilderness - that he might know what was in their heart. We none of us know how weak and sinful our heart is until we are brought face to face with temptation. We pride ourselves upon our purity, as white robes; but it may be we are pure only because we have never been subjected to the temptations which have blasted the lives and characters of others. We seem gentle and forgiving; but it may be that we have been sheltered from the vehemence of jealousy, envy, and hatred; have lived amongst those who have loved and honoured us; and have been undisputed monarchs in the little world of our life. We boast our honesty: but we have never known what it was to leave behind us in our homes a number of little children crying for bread, whilst all around plenty seemed strewn within our easy reach. It is not in Goshen with its flesh-pots and unstinted abundance, but in the wilderness where the supply of water fails, and the last crumb of bread is devoured, and the pressure of want crushes the soul - it is there that God knows what is in our heart, and our pretensions to nobility are tested to the uttermost.

But the third and main reason why God led the people through the wilderness was to suffer them to hunger. It may be that hunger had been comparatively unknown by them before they found themselves in the wilderness; and is it not a remarkable expression that God suffered them to hunger? Of course he could have so contrived that they had not hungered. The manna might have fallen before ever they came to Moses to murmur against him. The vast flocks of birds might have been carried on the wings of the wind within easy reach of their tents before the supplies which they brought with them from Egypt had been exhausted. But no, God suffered them to hunger. He had implanted the appetite for food; he knew how keen the pangs of hunger were, and yet he permitted them to suffer. How wonderful that God should let people suffer, and should put them into circumstances in which suffering is inevitable!

There is other and worse hunger than that for food. The hunger for love and sympathy! The hunger for a tone in a voice that is never heard! The hunger for the touch of a hand that is never felt! The hunger for opportunities of ministry that always elude the grasp! The hunger for congenial occupation, for knowledge, for travel, for refinement, art, beauty! God has implanted a strong desire for these things in our hearts, and yet he puts us into positions where there is no food, no answer, no satisfaction - nothing but the sense of a gnawing, aching desire.

Why is this? Partly, that we should learn that the true life after all does not depend upon the full supply of those foodstuffs which men deem so necessary, but upon something deeper, purer, diviner - God himself. He suffered them to hunger *that he might make them know*. In other words, had it not been for the hunger, Israel would not have known, and we should not know, what is revealed in the lack of all else. Life, which is life indeed, consists not in the abundance of things that we possess, but in knowing God, in having God, in being known and possessed by God, in receiving and feeding upon the words of God. Oh, blessed hunger, that drives the soul to God, and suddenly finds in God more than all. 'Man doth not live by bread only, but by every word that proceedeth from the mouth of God.'

We would not say one single word against accepting all innocent and right things that God puts into our life to meet the hunger implanted in our souls, but we affirm that, as it was with Jesus in the wilderness, so it is with many of his saints, who are chosen to close fellowship in his redemptive purpose, that ordinary supplies are cut off, in order that they may be driven to find the springs of life in God.

And what is it which really feeds

man's soul in the things that he so eagerly seeks? Is it not a divine quality which is in them, because they have come from God, as his gift, and as containing his thought? It must be possible, therefore, to derive from God himself at first hand and without intervention of any of these things, those qualities that are necessary to sustain and satisfy the soul. O hungry one, take thy hunger, of whatsoever kind it be, to God himself, and learn to find in him thy bread.

Then the manna came. All around the desert-camp there lay the small, round thing, freshly steeped in dew, and waiting to be gathered by the host. Beautiful in appearance; sweet to taste; prepared and ministered by angels. It was a rare gift, but Israel would never have known it, had they not first known hunger. God has something better for us than we fear. Not the leek or the onion, the garlic or the swine's flesh, but angels' food. Something so refined, so exquisite in its texture, so superabundant in its gladness, so divine in its quality, that it were better for us to have one meal of it a day in the desert than be in Paradise itself without it. Arise then, hungry pilgrim of the wilderness march, do not sit brooding in thy tent, eating out thy soul in thy despair, go forth unto God, unto God, thy exceeding joy. Take thy vessel with thee, and gather for thy need. If thou gather much thou shalt have none to spare, and if little, thou shalt have enough. 'Thou shalt eat and be satisfied, and bless the name of the Lord, who has dealt bountifully with thee', and God alone is enough.

Chapter 3

'There is a River!'

'There is a river, the streams whereof shall make glad the city of God, the holy place of the tabernacles of the most High' (Psalm 46:4).

A song by an unknown singer! Some son of Korah, borne on the tide of inspiration, uttered it in one of the darkest hours of his nation's history. It is evidently contemporaneous with Isaiah 33. The spirit of heroic faith that thrilled Isaiah had passed to some younger heart, and what in him was prophecy, in this was Psalm.

Sennacherib, with 200,000 of the cruelest soldiers that ever drew the sword, had crossed the northern frontier of Palestine, or had already stationed himself on the hills that were round about Jerusalem, intent on its capture and pillage. The virgin daughter of Zion was strongly fortified. Military skill had made the best possible use of the strong natural features of her position, and Jewish patriots had challenged their children to tell her towers, mark well her bulwarks, and consider her palaces, that they might tell the story to succeeding generations.

But there was one fatal defect, which invalidated all these advantages. Jerusalem was not well supplied with water. A deficient water supply! This meant disaster to the best concerted schemes of fortification and defence.

Dr Geikie gives an interesting account of the water supply of ancient Jerusalem. The only spring known to exist there rises beneath the ancient site of the Temple, and supplies what are known as the Fountain of the Virgin and the Pool of Siloam. This perennial supply of crystal water was, however, not sufficient to meet the requirements of such vast populations as crowded the city at the great festivals, and were driven thither, as at the time of which we write, by the pressure of invasion. Every effort was therefore made to augment the supply. There was a great system of subterranean tanks, forty to sixty feet deep, hewn out of the soft limestone, which underlay a harder rock on which the city was built. These were of great antiquity, and in one Jeremiah was confined. Vast cisterns were also built to catch and keep the rains. But, in addition, large pools, fed by aqueducts, were added outside the city and within. One aqueduct, built by Solomon, brought water from the Pools of Solomon beyond Bethlehem, and poured it into the huge reservoirs of the Temple area, a distance of thirteen miles. Hezekiah is also credited with having built yet another vast conduit, bringing the waters of Gihon straight to the west side of the city of David. In later days Herod the Great executed a marvellous work of the same kind.

All these efforts on the part of the citizens to remedy their water supply were a confession on their part to its deficiency, and afforded the ground for the perpetual iteration of the prophets that God himself would be to his people all that a river would have been in the abundance and freeness of its supplies.

'What!' said Isaiah, in one of his magnificent outbursts, 'do you require a river, whose flashing breadth would intercept the assault of the foe, and make it impossible for him to place battering-ram or scaling-ladder in immediate proximity to the walls? You need it not. The glorious Lord will be to us a place of broad river and streams. All around our city walls lies the engirding protection of the God of our fathers.'

'What!' said this son of Korah, 'do you want a supply of water to enable you to withstand the exigencies of the siege? All that will be yours in having God. He is not only around us; he is in the midst of us, and his presence, like a river, will make glad the city. Would you have a broad river pouring its translucent waters over the glistening pebbles, and purling in its majestic flow, supplying every cistern and garden with abundant water? This is yours in the Most High, who counts our city as the holy place of his tabernacle.'

Mr Rendel Harris classes the water supply of Jerusalem under four heads, and uses these as illustrating certain conditions of spiritual life, with which we are all familiar.

The Pool of Siloam represents the stagnation of those whose character and life show no signs of advance from year to year; always overcome by the same sins, reading the same chapters of the Bible, offering the same prayers.

The Pool of Bethesda stands for those whose life is intermittent. An angel comes down from time to time to trouble the waters, and for a while they possess and impart healing virtue, but the impulse is soon exhausted, and many a weary soul waits till the stirring comes again.

The Brook Kedron was fouled with the refuse of the city through which it flowed. It was, therefore, hardly fit to drink, though even today the water carriers fill their water-jars there. This represents such as mingle with their profession of Christianity much that is inconsistent and worldly.

The Aqueducts of Solomon recall the experience of many who are always depending for their religious life on the ministry of others. They do seek water from the distant hills, but they are somewhat too dependent on the teacher or conference or book by which it is brought within their reach.

Now all these classes of Christians are bidden to avail themselves of the River whose streams make glad the City of God. There is a sense in which the heavenly city has come down out of heaven from God. Our citizenship and conversation are there. There are times when, through our union with the living Saviour, we may say with the dying Payson: 'Its glories beam upon me, its breezes fan me, its odours are wafted to me, its sounds strike upon my ears, and its spirit is breathed into my heart'. These are the times when the river in full flow is passing before us, making us glad with the gladness which comes straight from the heart of the throne; and we are bidden, 'whosoever will', to take of the water of life freely. Not of the future only did the Apostle affirm that he saw a river of water of life, gleaming as crystal, proceeding out of the throne of God and of the Lamb, in the midst of the street of the New Jerusalem. Its source may be at the throne, but its waters have flowed down to earth, else how could men be so freely bidden to take?

Let us live by the river, fellow-believer, taking up its waters at any moment of need, just as the dwellers by the mighty Amazon or Congo go down to its vast supplies to help themselves without stint. They can afford to be extravagant, prodigal, wasteful! Is there not plenty? Can they not come again and again? Is there any fear of the reservoir of the hills running dry? Yet sooner might the Congo or Amazon become exhausted than thy God;

and sooner might the river remonstrate with the child for dipping its tin cup too frequently into its bosom, than the glorious Lord find fault with thy too incessant resort to him for his more abundant grace. Take! *Take*! **Take**! is Heaven's repeated invitation. 'Thou shouldest have smitten five or six times,' is God's bitter complaint.

There can be *no stagnation* where the river comes; it brings life with it, and deepens from the ankles to the knees, and from the knees to the loins, till its waters are a depth that cannot be waded through; and its current bears the soul forward irresistibly from grace to grace, from a superficial experience to the deep things of God, from the elements of the Gospel to the love that passeth understanding.

There can be *no intermittence*, as

when the waters need to be stored in some inner rock-chamber before they can gush out to their beneficent ministry, and, having exhausted themselves, retire to gather a fresh supply. This intermittent life is a very sad one, God-dishonouring and man-disappointing. There is something better when the soul is in perennial and abiding fellowship with Christ, by the Holy Spirit. Certainly there are freshets for us all, but these come on a full stream, and not on dry watercourses which have become heaps of stones. This maintained experience is only possible when care is taken over the early morning hours, and we can say with the Psalmist, 'Mine eyes are ever toward the Lord'.

There is *no pollution or impurity* in the religious life of those who drink of that river. Too often the religious observances of people are so mingled with the worldly show of some fashionable church, with the consciousness of being one of a gaily-dressed throng, or with the desire to do as others are doing, that the spirit is befouled in the act of drinking of the heavenly stream. There is all the difference between the waters that have flowed through a great city and those that issue from the hills. But if we live in God we are ever partaking of that crystal stream of pure and undefiled religion of which the apostle James speaks.

There is *no need of depending on human instrumentality.* We would not undervalue this - God has appointed it, and set his seal on it. But we must ever count it to be a means, and not an end. Some sculpture the arches of the aqueduct, and festoon them, and almost worship them in their senseless adulation. But they cannot quench the rage of the thirst-fever; they are liable to be broken down, or stopped up; they may at any moment cease affording their wonted supplies. Happy are they, therefore, who have learnt to go to the river for themselves, and to avail themselves at first-hand of its supplies.

The flow of the river is so *soft*; such a contrast to the tumult of the sea, which represents the rage of the foe. The waters roar and are troubled, the mountains shake with the swelling thereof. We can hear the dash of the wild waves, the emblem of unbridled power, of anarchy and fret and strife, of tumult and unrest. Such is the world, and such the wicked, who are like the troubled sea when it cannot rest. What a relief to turn to the gentle murmur of the river, whose waters glide in musical ripple along their banks. The greatest and best things, in nature and human life and God, are stillest.

The flow of the river is so *bountiful*. 'The streams thereof' are the *divisions* thereof; as when each Egyptian ryot along the Nile draws off its waters by the tiny canal into his piece of garden ground, or when our house-pipes tap the mains. 'Unto each one of us was the grace given according to the measure of the gift of Christ.' 'The same Spirit divides to each one severally even as he will.'

The flow of the river is so *gladdening*. There is the gladness of perfect satisfaction, of security against possible need, of peace that passeth understanding, of the infinite repose of the soul when it has found its rest. The scorching drought may bake the hills around, till the landscape pants and faints, and every hill is a reflector, and every valley a furnace; but the soul which has learnt to avail itself of God is glad, because it thirsts not; it has become like a garden, whose waters fail not.

This river is the blessed Spirit. He is gentle; he is pure and holy, clear as crystal; he is bountiful. Out of him who receives the Spirit, Jesus said, 'shall flow rivers of living water'. He is joy-giving and glad-making. He proceeds from the Father and the Son, and with them is to be honoured and glorified. It was only when the Lamb had gone to the throne that the Spirit could be given. Directly the Second Person of the Holy Trinity took his seat at the right hand of the Father, as a lamb which had been slain, there poured out, as from the smitten rock of the wilderness, the abundant river whose first head was Pentecost, its second Samaria, its third Ephesus, and its fourth perhaps will be not far distant, close beside the end of the present age.

At the beginning of Genesis we read of the river that watered the garden, and became four heads. This was an emblem of things that were to come. Already the substance has been given, in part perhaps as yet, but destined to ever fuller and richer manifestation until the perfect realisation of its entire significance in the ages which are awaiting the summons of their King.

In the meanwhile, fellow-believer, in the absence of all that others boast themselves of possessing, be sure that there is a river; be sure to find its banks, and live there; make much of the Holy Ghost, as he speaks in Scripture, and breathes through the open casement of the soul.

Chapter 4

The Soul's True Affinity

'Know ye not, brethren, (for I speak to them that know the law) how that the law hath dominion over a man as long as he liveth?

For the woman which hath an husband is bound by the law to her husband so long as he liveth; but if the husband be dead, she is loosed from the law of her husband.

So then if, while her husband liveth, she be married to another man, she shall be called an adulteress: but if her husband be dead, she is free from that law; so that she is no adulteress, though she be married to another man.

Wherefore, my brethren, ye also are

become dead to the law by the body of Christ; that ye should be married to another, even to him who is raised from the dead, that we should bring forth fruit unto God.

For when we were in the flesh, the motions of sins, which were by the law, did work in our members to bring forth fruit unto death.

But now we are delivered from the law, that being dead wherein we were held; that we should serve in newness of spirit, and not in the oldness of the letter (Romans 7:1-6).

Beneath the strong rugged thought which runs through chapters 6 and 7 of the Epistle to the Romans, we do not always detect the tender little allegory which connects the two. It is perhaps more than an allegory, for earthly relationships are probably patterns of things in the heavens, and there are correspondences linking the inward with the outward, the unseen and eternal with the temporal and seen.

When we are awakened from the lethargy and death of sin to seek after and realise the Divine ideal which calls to us, *we are first attracted towards God's holy law.* If only we may enter into alliance with it, we suppose that we shall easily attain whatsoever things are true, pure, lovely, and of good report. We are strongly drawn to it. As it looks out on us from the ten words of Sinai, speaks to us in the voice of conscience, or is reflected from the pages of a Marcus Aurelius or Epicetus, we are fascinated by its beauty. It is as when the traveller for the first time sees the touch of dawn on a line of snow-clad Alps, struck out sharp against the deep azure of heaven.

The law is holy, just, and good. We delight in it after the inward man. Our judgment approves it, our reason vindicates it, our conscience bears witness to it, our sense of the fitness of things acknowledges its claims. We are able to love it with all our mind, if not with all our heart. And it seems to us that by constant companionship we shall necessarily become transformed into its sublime and heavenly likeness. The soul deems that it has found its true affinity. There is the dawn of a new joy, the flush of a new hope.

But this experience is destined to be short-lived. There is a fundamental incongruity in the alliance. It is not that the law is deficient in any of those qualities with which the soul's thought had invested it, but that there is an everlasting incompatibility between its holiness and the manifold weakness and sinfulness of the flesh. The law is spiritual, but we are carnal; the law is perfect, we are sold under sin; the law is heavenly, we are of the earth, earthly. And thus the soul becomes aware of its awful mistake, cries out in the bitterness of its anguish, and sighs for deliverance and relief. The dye of its sinfulness seems even deeper and darker, because it works death by that which is good. The deceitfulness of the flesh appears more inveterate, because it takes occasion by the commandment to work all manner of concupiscence. And yet it seems as though nothing can happen to free the soul from its union with the law it has espoused.

At this point, when the blackness of despair has settled down on the hopes and anticipations which the soul had so fondly cherished, *it awakes to discover new and unrealised depths of meaning in the Cross*. It sees its sinful flesh nailed there in effigy and likeness. It realises that we who believe have become dead to the law by the body of Christ. It understands, that as death intervenes between husband and wife, dissolving their union by removing one into another sphere so that each is free of the other, similarly the death of Christ, in which we were identified, has placed the law and ourselves in different spheres, the law being left in the earth-sphere, whilst we have risen into the heavenly and eternal one, and thus we are freed from the law, 'having died to that wherein we were held, that we should serve in newness of spirit, and not in the oldness of the letter'.

It is a blessed thing when we apprehend this side of our Saviour's death. It is *for* sin certainly; but it is also *unto* sin. We become dead to the law by the body of Christ. It is the release of death: and the soul, with thankful gladness, knows that the bonds by which it was bound to a relationship it could not sustain is for ever at an end. The law is not dead, or abrogated, or abolished, but its hold on the soul, as a means of justification and sanctification, is for ever at an end. There can therefore be no charge of disloyalty or unfaithfulness, even though it be married to another.

Then, in this new glad life, on Easter

soil, as a child of the Resurrection, and admitted into the realm of the Infinite and Eternal, *the soul comes on its true affinity*, in which it can meet with neither disappointment nor dissatisfaction. It encounters the risen Christ, in whom it recognises him that died in weakness on the Cross, but now lives for ever in power and glory, and all its nature leaps towards him as its true Spouse and Home. All that attracted it before in the law is in him. Was it holy, just, and good? So is he! Did it elicit a response from judgment, conscience, and sense of fitness? So does he! But he has qualities the law never possessed. He can forgive; he has grace to help in time of need. He makes no appeal for the obedience of the self-life, but promotes the obedience which he demands. He lifts us into a new sphere, secures death to self and sin, and indwells by the power of the Holy Ghost.

None can impute to him any connivance with our imperfections, frailties, and sins. They cost him agony, blood, tears, death. There is on his part no weak yielding of the lofty ideal which seems to mock us, as we lie paralysed at its base. The standard of Christ, which is that of Love, is more searching and comprehensive than that of Law. The spirit asks for more than the letter. But his love begets in us the love that possesses and energises the soul; his death involves death to sinful passions, and to the law as a means of righteousness; his Spirit frees us from the power of the self-life, and fashions us by imperceptible but certain stages into the likeness of his glory.

The Old Version says we are *married* to another; the Revised Version renders it *joined* to another; the original says simply *should be* for another. What sublimity lurks in this simplicity! In life and death, by day and night, in the busy haunts of toil, and in its repose, to be always and only for that other, that glorious Man, in whom truth and mercy have met, righteousness and peace have kissed. All difficulties resolve themselves when brought to this touchstone. The eye is single, and the whole body is full of light. All sin becomes personal disloyalty and infidelity to the gentlest and truest of Friends. All life is animated by the purpose of an absorbing love, that yearns for nothing so much as to set forth the praises of him who fills the entire horizon of the soul. Thus we bring forth fruit unto God.

The Apostle uses a very strong word to describe *the service which love promotes*. He says that we *serve* in newness of the spirit, and not in the oldness of the letter (7:6). It is the service of the slave. There is no slavery so absolute as that of love. To promote the wellbeing of the loved one is the one aim and purpose of existence. The fetters never hurt wrist or ankle, because there is no disposition to be rebellious or turn away back. Love prompts the heart to move in perfect accord with the demands that the strictest law might formulate. But before law calls, love answers, and every need is anticipated before it has time to assert itself. The strings of daisies which are threaded by a child's fingers on the spring-lawns will compel its mother, with an immediateness and imperativeness which iron and steel could not secure.

It is thus that the Divine law is not annulled, but established through the work of Christ. Not only does he magnify it and make it honourable by his own obedience unto death, but he secures its supremacy in the hearts of those who are joined to him by faith, and receive of his Spirit. What the law could not do in that it was weak through the flesh, is done through the Son himself. The righteousness of the law is fulfilled in us, who walk not after the flesh, but after the Spirit.

But we must be very careful not to take advantage of God's free grace. The greater our privileges, the deeper our responsibility. To whom much is given, of such will more be required. Love is very exacting in its claims, quick in its instincts, awful in its jealousy. Let us avoid giving needless pain to our faithful Lover, Christ.

Chapter 5

Christ One and Manysided

'In that day sing ye unto her, A vineyard of red wine'
(Isaiah 27:2).

Life presents the same features to the toiling myriads of England as to the dwellers amid the vineyards and pasture lands of Judah, to whom Isaiah wrote when he compared it to the experiences of a caravan passing across a sandy waste. Sometimes it is the sirocco blast of temptation, burning hot; the air is laden with particles of grit that sting and irritate, and find their way through closed doors; thus all day long the devil vexes us. Sometimes the tempest of trouble rises high; the cavillings and misjudgments of men, difficulties in daily business, the overwhelming competition and strife of our time, combine to fill our lives with storm. Now we happen on a dry place, from which human love seems to have retreated, so that no green thing breaks the monotony of our pilgrimage, no child's embrace, no tender caress, no tone or touch of love. And, again, we are traversing a weary land; we are tired, tired of the inward strife, of the daily cross, of the perpetual demand on our sympathy and self-control, longing for the evening bell, and the passage across the harbour-bar from the restless sea to the tranquil waters of the haven.

We must not take the pessimist's view of life. In every year there are more hours of sun than of rain, in all lives there are more joys than sorrows. For all grief there is an anodyne: for all loss there is compensation. Nature is always beautiful. Troops of fresh young lives are ever pouring into our world, with their merry laughter and their gay frolic. The very work of life brings zest and interest; and hope is ever painting its bright frescoes on the dark cloud that hides the future. And yet it is undeniable that there are many sad aspects to life which press themselves upon our notice, and sometimes cause heart and flesh to fail.

Men naturally resort to the readiest methods of averting the pressure of anxiety and pain. The natural man is always looking out for his hiding-place, the niche in the rock which may serve as one. He resorts to a temporary expedient which serves him in pressing difficulty; but shortly after he is seeking for a covert against a tornado, which suddenly has broken upon him. After a while he is sensible of consuming thirst, and searches in another direction for water. And again worn by fatigue he looks around for a great rock, casting a sharply-defined shadow on the burning sand, in whose blue depths he may find shelter. Thus man is always seeking help in different quarters to carry him through the pressing anxieties and difficulties of his life.

The children of this world hide themselves under the golden canopy of money, which wards off many of the grosser forms of evil, but cannot satisfy the craving of the heart for love and sympathy and rest. They yield themselves to systems of philosophy that brace men to suffer with stoical fortitude and indifference, as when the weak and boneless animal makes for itself the hard shell or case that shelters it from collision and shock. Or they take refuge in some passionate human attachment, seeking in man or woman the covert, the water-spring, and the shadow of a great rock; a hope which is doomed to disappointment, because none is all-sided enough to supply another's need in the numberless necessities of human experience. These are broken cisterns, clouds without rain, the mirage without the fountain, the grate without fire.

In all true life there is education and growth. We pass upward from *things* to human sympathy, and seek in men and women the comforter we originally sought in wealth, or travel, or book. Then we pass from the outward to the inward, from the finite to the infinite, from the time sphere to the eternal. We start back appalled at the insufficiency of the tenderest human love to meet the exhaustless hunger of our souls, and long for the Divine in human form, presented to us in the Man. Finally there comes a great unity into our life, and having found the Man in whom all the fulness of the Godhead dwells, having realised something of what he can be to the soul that he made and redeemed, we return again to men and things, and find in them a beauty and fitness which we had never realised before. Nature wears a lovelier dress, because the Man, whom we love, arrayed her, and her hues and scents are borrowed from his thought. Children are lovelier, because they reflect traits of his character. All true thoughts are more satisfying, because we detect in them the intonations of his voice. Earthly friendships are transfigured, because as we lift them to our lips they brim with water from the fountain of his love; and the commonest incidents of life are invested with unwonted meaning, because all things are of him, and through him, and to him for ever.

For the Christian, only one Being is needful. There is a blessed unity in his life. He desires only the Man of whom Isaiah spoke, the Man that trod the soil of Palestine, that died upon the cross, that lives in the glory, the Man Christ Jesus. Jesus is the one answer to every question, the one satisfaction of every desire. To the Apostles the

Master was all in all. In him they found strength for spiritual conflict, defence from their foes, tenderness amid rebuke and reproach, rest in weariness; and Jesus Christ is willing to be as much and more to all who believe on him through their word. During his earthly life, he was the one answer to all the aches and ills of human bodies. Blindness, paralysis, demon possession, found their antidote in his presence, his name, his touch. And he is still all-sufficient to meet each demand now of the spiritual, as then of the physical life.

All we require for this life and the next is ours in Christ. We are, alas, too slow to possess our possessions. Do we need a shelter from the sirocco of temptation? We may find it in Jesus. Hiding behind him, taking refuge in the pavilion of his Presence, we are secure. Put the Man Christ Jesus between you and temptation or adverse circumstances, as the Roman soldier his shield between him and the fiery darts of the foe. In days of tempest he is the impenetrable covert. In loneliness he is like the murmur of waters in a dry place. In weariness he is the shadow of a great rock, beneath which we may sit with great delight. In other words Jesus Christ is the one answer of the soul to every possible circumstance, to all emergencies, to the demands and appeals that constantly knock at the door of our life, like the telegraph lad with the buff-coloured envelope, and its unexpected summons.

There is something more. The soul that abides in Christ extracts blessings from the repeated discipline which reveals the many-sidedness of Christ. It greets sirocco and tornado; it welcomes drought and weariness; it rejoices in tribulation; because out of all these things it is acquiring an experience of qualities and attributes which otherwise had slumbered in Christ unknown. Human need has always been the background for the revelation of God's nature, as the ailments of a child reveal the tender patience of the mother, and as the virulence of disease the resource of doctor or nurse. You ask to know him, then be not surprised if you are placed on steep standpoints of vision whence unexpected glimpses of his nature may be obtained.

Not unfrequently men teach us what the Man can be. They are but broken lights of him. Splinters from the crystal, drops from the fountain. One setting forth this trait, and another that of his character, but none of them able to combine more than one, or at the most two, of those characteristics which the prophet attributes to the Man whose praises he recites. They are coverts, but not hiding-places; or hiding-places, but not rivers; or rivers, but not shadowing rocks. Take the best of the best of men; gather into one all the chivalry, bravery, tenderness, loveliness, which have dwelt in the fairest of our race; and all together will not suffice to depict the comprehensiveness, and glory, and sufficiency of the Son of Man.

It should be our ambition so to live that men may catch glimpses of Christ in us, so that they may say, if this man or this woman is so strong and sweet, so true and tender, what must not he be, in whom their virtues dwell as their home? And for ourselves, such may be our fellowship with Christ, that we shall be less sensitive to the transitions and trials of our mortal life. There shall be no more sirocco, or waterless waste, or unbearable heat, because in having him, we shall be shielded in him. These great modern cities will become in our eyes as fair as lands of perennial spring; and sad, homeless, desolate hearts become more sensible of their possessions than of their losses, of the One Presence than of the absence of any. 'Our sun shall no more go down, neither shall our moon withdraw itself, for the Lord shall be to us an everlasting light, and the days of our mourning shall be ended.'

Chapter 6

How to Become Like Christ

'But we all, with open face beholding as in a glass the glory of the Lord, are changed into the same image from glory to glory, even as by the Spirit of the Lord' (2 Corinthians 3:18).

Many are seeking the true policy of life. But in all directions there is perplexity and confusion; either men are living at haphazard or are adopting a policy dictated by selfishness and worldly wisdom. On all sides the question is being asked, What is life? Whither is the hurrying current bearing us? How shall we make the best of the short interval between the cradle and the grave? What thread of all the many that offer themselves to our hand will conduct us through the labyrinth with its darkness into the light? 'What shall we do?' is a question often put.

The clue to life's aims; the philosopher's stone which will turn everything into gold; the secret of a blessed useful life is to be found much rather in what we *are*, than in what we *do*. The Beatitudes with which our Lord opened the great programme of Christianity all turn upon character rather than upon action, and the blessedness which he promises is to the meek, the pure in heart, the peacemaker. The true policy of life, therefore, is to stay just where we are; to believe that to be what and where we are is God's will for us; and to endeavour to be the noblest, sweetest, purest, strongest possible. Not to fret because the sphere is obscure; not to be jealous of the position occupied by others; not to allow the peace of the inner life to be broken by the feverish desire to be something else; but to be quiet, evincing all that nobility of disposition and character which the opportunity and occasion call for. For men to be strong, thoughtful, considerate of women and of the weak, tender to little children, self-controlled, able to command the tides that sweep through heart and thought. For women to be pure and devout, gentle and modest, adorned with the jewels of the meek and quiet spirit, which in God's sight is of great price; and to be this constantly, in days of fog as well as of sunshine, of illness as of buoyant strength; this surely will extract from the roughest and most toilsome path the largest amount of blessedness that this world can give.

John Stuart Mill was accustomed to say that whenever the path of his life was not clear, he was accustomed to ask what Jesus of Nazareth would probably have done under the same circumstances, and that the test never failed to indicate the true course to adopt; and for us there is surely no higher ideal of life than to ask perpetually - What would Jesus do were he in my place? Each one of us must have an ideal by which to mould our life, and there is no such ideal as that presented to us in the life of our blessed Lord. To be like Christ is to know something of the joy and peace that perennially filled his heart.

There is a great necessity that we should be all this, because knowledge depends on character; we know, only when we are willing to do his will. The light of the morning will only illumine our mind when we have followed the narrow path of obedience up the steep ascent of righteousness and truth. Many ask what is the right policy of life with the intention of being nobler and purer so soon as they clearly see how to live. Such are destined to disappointment. The only solution to life's many problems is to begin at once, just where we are, to be what God demands of us, assured that soon we shall learn all that he would teach us.

But how can we become Christlike? The answer is given in a significant text which has been illuminated with a new beauty in the Revised Version - 'We all with unveiled face, *reflecting as a mirror* the glory of the Lord, are transformed into the same image, from glory to glory'.

We all. There is no monopoly in the religion of Jesus Christ. Its doors stand open for all who will enter. No inner circle, no privileged class, no school of initiates. What was possible for Moses in the old dispensation, and for him alone, is free to us all, to the rank and file of the Church as well as to the Apostles, to the eighteenth century as well as the first.

With unveiled face. We are told that Moses veiled his face, partly because the people could not stand its dazzling light, and partly because he wished to hide from them its dwindling glory (verse 13). And his veil was afterwards spread upon the hearts of the Jews, who could not see the spiritual beauty of their own law, because they were hardened. But there must be no veil of prejudice, or unbelief, or permitted sin upon the face which is turned towards the Son of God. With the clear undimmed gaze of purity and truth, we must look into his.

Reflecting as a mirror. In the older version, 'Beholding as in a glass', which had a helpful and deep significance; but surely this is even yet more helpful, as it is truer to the Apostle's phrase. We are to reflect Jesus as the mirror does the face and movements of the person in whose apartment it stands. Silent and unobtrusive; constantly and faithfully, it reflects every gesture; so the Christian heart should live in daily, hourly fellowship with the face of Jesus Christ. As the eyes of servants are to the hand of their master, so our eyes should be directed towards and our lives perpetually reflecting our Lord, whom the world cannot see, but who is ever present to the eye of our faith.

As Jesus looks into our lives, in their pellucid depths he should see his own face reflected. Yea, as God the Father looks down upon us he should see a faithful reflection of his Son. And as the giddy world around casts casual glances at the people of God they should be arrested, not so much by what they say as by the features of the Master which they present. Perhaps each unit in the Church is needed to mirror to the world some trait or feature of Emmanuel. Each believer should daily ask himself, 'What do my companions and associates see of Christ in me?' and the supreme test of every action should be, 'How can I so conduct myself as to reveal some trait of my Master's character?' Whatever it may cost it should be the ambition of each lover of Christ to transmit perpetually the beauty of the Lord, so that others may admire him in them that believe.

Ask how Christ is acting; always repeat what he is doing; do nothing of yourself; whatsoever he doeth do it likewise; make all things of the pattern shown to the eye of faith upon the Mount; act thus, not because you wish to, or like to, or feel pleasure in it, but because you ought, and thus instinctively, and unconsciously you will really become like Christ. The likeness of Christ will pass from the outward act and speech, in which there may be some effort, to the inner temper and disposition of the soul. Put on the Lord Jesus Christ by daily appropriating the grace of his character, and that grace will become indigenous to the soul of your heart.

We are transformed. This is the word used of the Transfiguration of Christ. We too shall have a transfiguration; not as his, a sudden and immediate change, but one that will grow on us from day to day, too gradual to be noticed save by comparisons that stretch over years. Act like Christ, and you will increasingly come to think and feel like him.

But none of this is possible save by the grace of the Holy Spirit. He first implants the desire for the holy life, and leads us to live nearer Christ, and enables us to resemble him, and works in us the inward temper and disposition. From beginning to end the grace of the Christian life is due to the Blessed Spirit, and when once he takes the soul in hand, there is no fear that the work will retrograde or be dimmed, as the light that faded from the face of Moses; rather it will proceed, by insensible degrees, from glory to glory, and we shall see in each other more and more of the character and beauty of the Risen and Ascended Master.

But there is something yet to be said. The Lord Jesus is in the heart of each believer, by the grace of the Holy Spirit. The perfect image may be in embryo, wrapped up as a forest tree in acorn or seed, but it is certainly present. And each time we are called upon to resemble Christ, to act or speak as he would have done, to reflect him to men, we have to deal not only with the Christ of the throne, but the Christ of the heart. Let us make way, so that the Christ in us may speak or act through us; so that the image without may be reproduced, not simply by reflection, but by indwelling and outshining.

Chapter 7

The Immanence of Christ

Our religion is deeper than is commonly supposed. It is a great loss in every way that we are accustomed to speak of faith in Christ, forgiveness, and cleansing from sin as if they were the crown and climax of Christianity, instead of being its outworks, its outer-courts, the staircases and corridors to its throne-room, its reparative processes preparatory to its essential life and heart. Christianity fails of its chief end in any life that it affects, unless it produces there, so far as may be possible, the life of the Eternal God himself, as it is resident in Jesus Christ and communicated by the Holy Spirit.

In regeneration, at whatever time it takes place, and under whatever circumstances, the principle of a new life is inserted in the human spirit. As the animal has a higher life than the plant, and as man, in his moral nature, has a higher life than the animal, so the man who has been regenerated by the Spirit of God has become possessed of a life to which the ordinary man can lay no claim. He has become, as the Apostle Peter puts it, 'a partaker of the Divine nature'. Whatever be our differences as to creed or Church, they are comparatively unimportant, so long as we possess within our spirits this Divine life, which is Christ in us, the hope of glory. 'Know ye not,' said the Apostle, as though it were an anomaly to be ignorant of this primal fact, 'that Jesus Christ is in you, except ye be reprobates?'

The whole scheme of redemption, the entire work of Jesus Christ, his birth in which he brought the Divine under the conditions of the human, his death by which he acquired power to pass it on, his resurrection and ascension through which he bore it regnant and triumphant to the throne, his gift of the Holy Spirit by which he makes it available to all who believe - *all* tend to this as their flower and fruit, that he should reproduce himself in us. And if year by year we are not becoming more pure and strong and Christ-like, we may gravely question whether we have not deceived ourselves in thinking that we have received him into our nature.

The true seat of the Divine indwelling is the spirit. We are rather lax in our use of terms, and fail to divide between soul and spirit. In clear and accurate thinking on these deep matters we should conceive of the soul as the seat of the ego, of our individuality, and of all the attributes of thought and love, of hope and imagination, with which we are endowed; but the spirit in man is the Holy of Holies of his nature, the inner shrine, the natural residence and resort of the Spirit of God, with whom it has a native affinity. We worship God in the spirit. Probably the heart is the Hebrew correlative in the Old Testament of the spirit in the New.

There, in the spirit of man, in depths below the play of self-consciousness and energy and emotion, in the temple of the inner life, the Divine life literally dwells. Strengthened by might through the Spirit in the inner man, Christ dwells in our hearts by faith; and as the discipline of life proceeds he is increasingly formed within us. It is a great moment in a man's life when this conception first breaks on him, or to adopt the Apostle's phrase, when God reveals it to him. He suddenly awakens to the fact that he has within him that eternal life which was in the Father, and was manifested to the world in his Son, and is now communicated by the Spirit. Bitter and deep are the regrets that he has not recognised it before, that he has been too monopolised by the play of his own life to give way to its holy promptings and inspirations. It is as though a man who for years has been working some heavy machinery by handpower, at great strain and cost to himself, should suddenly awake to find that in his factory for years there has been a handle which, had he but touched it, would have connected his machine with a powerful dynamo, and would have saved him all his expenditure.

We must distinguish between the conception of the Christ-ideal, or the enthusiasm of the Christ-spirit, and the literal indwelling of the Son of God, through the Holy Spirit. In all ages the minds of men have been sensitive to influences like these. Some lofty ideal, like that of the Virgin Mother, which inspired the knight-errants of the Middle Ages; some Divine enthusiasm, like that which led the rich and high-born to abjure all that they might resemble Christ in his lowliness and poverty - such lofty inspirations have visited and possessed men, nerving them to sublime and heroic lives. But these do not fulfil the measure of this conception, that Christ is actually resident in the regenerated soul. They may proceed from that indwelling, but they have existed apart from it, and in comparison with it they are as artificial flowers to the exquisite texture and fragrance of the sweet nurselings of spring.

We cannot understand it. It is, as St Paul says, a great mystery. But then all life is mysterious, and whatever is connected with God is mysterious to us. We might well question whether our religion were of God, if it did not touch on regions of mystery, if its paths did not after a while become tracks on the illimitable expanse of his being, presently fading from view. But we have all learnt to distinguish between mysteries we cannot solve and facts we gladly recognise and accept. We know not what life is. We sit beside our dying friend until the death-rattle or the gentle sigh announces that life is gone, but what is it that goes out? What is the life which we possess when we live, and lose when we die? These are questions we cannot answer, but we still accept the fact of life throbbing within ourselves or our fellows. And thus we think of the mystery of Christ's indwelling; it baffles thought or speech, but we reverently accept it as a fact, and as we do so we find that it explains many another fact in our own consciousness, and in the history of the Church. It should, however, be our aim to yield to this life as far as possible. We must not be content with knowing that within the chambers of our heart there dwells this Mysterious Guest, in whom all wisdom and strength and love reside; we must often tread the corridors that lead to his apartment, consult with him, interchange ideas and thoughts, lay before him our intentions, purposes, and plans; nay, we must ask him to step forth into the dwelling of the soul, tenanting every room, and affecting even the members of the body with the glow and radiance of his presence.

Two things are needful before we can realise the full benefit of this indwelling:

(1) *We must curtail the manifestation of our own energy.* This is by no means easy. Our Lord spoke of it as the daily cross, as laying down our lives, as losing our very souls, for the

word translated *soul* is really life. We fight hard to hold our own; we have planned, managed, wrought so long that we are inapt in reining in our self-life, so that the Christ-life may become dominant. We are willing enough to adopt any theory of life that gives foothold to the spirit of self still to keep the government of our lives in its hands, such as the rightness of strict obedience to the law and spirit of Christ. We are willing that he should be constitutional monarch, if only a religious self may be his executive.

But whatever partakes of *self* is inimical to our true interests. We must stand aside. There cannot be two dominant principles within us. One must give way. John the Baptist must decrease if Christ is to increase. The marble must be chipped off if the fashion of the image is to grow. The first Adam, who is but a living soul, must give place to the second Adam, who is a life-giving spirit.

All this needs constant watchfulness. Whenever we are sensible of the forth-putting of energy, we must be on the alert that its source should not be self, but Christ; and that its one purpose should be to manifest him more perfectly, and to attract to him more of the admiration and love of men. There is no merit in the deepest self-denial. We do not lop off the branches, shoots, and tendrils of our own life because of any virtue in the act, but only to curtail anything that might drain the energies of our nature away from the Christ graft, or interfere to the least degree with the manifestation of Christ's own royal and glorious Being.

(2) *We must have times of silence, of waiting only upon God,* of retiring from the murmur and hubbub of human voices, that the still, small voice may be able to make itself heard. Such hours are not lost. We are arrested from taking paths which otherwise we should have to retrace with slow and weary steps. We escape the useless expenditure of energy which we might better conserve. We become conscious of the rising up within of that great fountain of life, which, having come from God, proceeds to God, and that bears us forward, like Mary, to do the one great act of self-sacrifice which lives when the many things of the bustling Martha life are forgotten.

It may not be necessary literally to sit still, or to go apart from the ordinary avocations of life, in order to detect this voice. The boiler-makers can talk to each other amid ceaseless hammerings. Those who are accustomed to the roar of Niagara are sensitive to noises that would not be audible to the unaccustomed ear. So, when once we have caught the tone of the voice of God, we shall detect it amid the rush of daily business. We shall make a great stillness in our heart, enter the inner temple, and wait there, until the word of the Lord shall come to us; and all the while to the eyes of our fellows we shall be busy with the occupations and amenities of life.

The one aim, however, of existence should be to give an opportunity to the indwelling Lord to assert himself, and possess the entire realm of spirit, soul and body, so that we may in our measure be able to say with the Apostle, 'Daily delivered to death for Jesus' sake, that the life of Jesus may be manifest in our mortal flesh'.

Chapter 8

The Other Advocate

'And I will pray the Father, and he shall give you another Comforter, that he may abide with you for ever'
(John 14:16).

'Another Comforter', or Paraclete, the Master said. The Church has two Advocates - the one with the Father in heaven, Jesus Christ the Righteous, the other in her midst, for 'we have been builded together as an habitation of God through the Spirit'. 'Ye,' said the Apostle, speaking of the Church collectively, 'are the temple of the Holy Ghost.' When the one Advocate went up, the other came down to be to each believer, and to the whole

Church, all that the Lord Jesus would have been had the ministry of the forty days been indefinitely prolonged. This is the secret of prayer; by the Spirit in the heart we are brought into living sympathy with the Saviour on the throne, and we naturally ask those things which it is the will of God to give.

There is a remarkable parallel between the Advents of the Second and Third Persons of the Holy Trinity. The Lord Jesus was, of course, in existence before his incarnation; yea, more, his delights were with the sons of men, and he wrought amongst them as the Angel-Jehovah; but at Bethlehem he entered into union with our nature. So the Holy Spirit wrought in the hearts of holy men before the Day of Pentecost, moving them to write the Scriptures, and to do great deeds of holy courage, but at Pentecost in an especial manner, he entered into union with the Church. What the manger-bed was to the one, the upper room was to the other. And now the Holy Spirit is as certainly immanent in the Body of which Christ is Head, as Jesus was immanent in the Body born of the Virgin Mother.

Of course, as the Church is made up of individual believers, the immanence of the Divine Spirit in the whole depends on his immanence in each. And his indwelling in any individual spirit is necessarily productive of all manner of Christ-forming, sin-destroying, grace-producing results. Holiness is the inevitable outcome of the indwelling of the Holy Ghost when he is permitted entire and undisputed supremacy. Of these our space forbids more than this mere mention, as we wish only to enumerate the special functions of the Spirit of God in respect of the Church's mission in the world.

The Anointing Function

Here, too, there is a remarkable parallel between the experiences of Christ and of his Church. Not only was he conceived of the Holy Ghost, but when the long preparatory period had passed, he was anointed for his work as the great Servant of God. He stooped to associate himself with sinners by submitting to baptism in the swellings of Jordan, and immediately the Spirit of God, who had been *in* him, descended *upon* him, and he was able to say, 'The Spirit of the Lord is upon me, because he hath anointed me to preach'. This was our Saviour's Pentecost, the hour in which he was endued with power, and was filled by the Spirit, not by measure, but in illimitable abundance.

Similarly, when the Church which, so to speak, had been conceived of the Holy Ghost, was essaying to undertake her great mission to the world, to preach the Gospel to the poor, to proclaim liberty to the captive, the opening of the prison to the bound, she, too, was anointed for her work. Not a step might she stir, though the world was knocking at her doors, till she had been thus endued with power from on high.

Ever since then the Risen Christ has been anointing and enduing men. The oil which has been so copiously poured on the head of our Aaron descends to each fragment of his sacred dress that claims the sacred chrism. The Lord received the Holy Ghost as an individual at the Jordan, but he received him again, so Peter tells us, when he ascended up on high, and this time as our Head and Representative (Acts 2:33). He has been infilled that he may infill; anointed that he may anoint; endued that he may endue. Though in all this it must be remembered that we are not now touching on his Divine Nature, but on his office as the High Priest of his Church. As a river pouring over a mountain-side fills the large tarns and lakes below, so the nature of God pours into the Divine human nature of the Son, and so by the Spirit into all hearts that by faith claim his infilling.

His Administering Function

Throughout the Book of Acts, we find that the Holy Ghost is the prime mover and administrator. *He* said to Peter, 'Three men seek for thee, go with them, I have sent them'; *He* said, 'Separate me Barnabas and Saul'; *He* controlled the movements of the Apostle, 'the Spirit of Jesus suffered them not'; *He* was so evidently present in the Church, that the first official document ran thus: 'It seemed good to the Holy Ghost, and to us'. He struck down those that lied against his Divine Majesty. These are instances out of many. Indeed, there is not a chapter in the Acts which does not contain some reference to the administrative function of the Holy Ghost.

And what was true of the early Church has been true in the history of the universal Church in every age, and might be true of each separate one. My beloved friend, the late Dr Gordon, to long talks with whom on this subject I owe so much, once told me that in his earlier ministry he was more anxious to administer and guide his church than in later years. He found that he was attempting work which the Holy Spirit could do better. It was enough, therefore, to preach perpetually on the work of the Holy Spirit, to keep his people's minds directed towards it, and to believe that the Spirit himself would energise through the church to the perfect realising of all its possibilities.

The Co-operating Function
A scientific lecturer often employs the services of a demonstrator, who,

by the experiments he performs, or the figures he chalks on the blackboard, presents to the eye what the speaker is presenting to the ear. This co-operation is like the double lens of the binocular glass, and the impression of the conjoint witness is proportionately great. So, ever since the day of Pentecost, when a servant of Christ has stood up in the right condition of soul and in believing fellowship with the Divine Spirit, he has been a fellow-witness to the Gospel. 'We are witnesses of these things, and *so is also the Holy Ghost.*'

Whilst the servant of God is elaborating and enforcing the truth disclosed to him through the Bible, at the moment that he is speaking the Spirit of God is at work, convicting of sin, righteousness, and judgment, demonstrating the truth of what is advanced, and driving the arrow home in the joints of the harness. It is a mistake, therefore, to argue for the Gospel; it is better far to bear witness to it. This is our function. 'Ye shall be witnesses unto me.' But it is highly important that we present Christ in his Gospel. The Spirit is not bound to add his testimony to aught else. Not to bursts of eloquence, nor to reams of essays on the last strike, nor to philosophy and science, but to the truth as it is in Jesus, is the Spirit responsive.

If once a man learns to rely on this, it makes him wonderfully calm and still. His fury and passion will not affect his purpose, but if he really knows 'the communion', or partnership, 'of the Holy Spirit', that will answer all.

His Upbuilding Function

Between the first and second Advents God is forming a new humanity. The Head was constituted in the Incarnation, but especially in the death and resurrection of the Second Adam. The Body is being added, soul by soul. It is worth our while to give full meaning to the phrase, 'Believers were the more *added to the Lord*' (Acts 5:14). They were, of course, added to the Church, but before that they had been added to the Lord. They were added to the Church because they had been added to the Lord.

This is a special function of the Holy Spirit to attract and draw men to the Head. He does this through the Church. Thus the Body of Christ is being built up. In the purpose of God we may say, as David did of his natural body, 'In thy book all my members were written, which in continuance were fashioned'. That is the point; the members of the Lord's mystical body are being fashioned *in continuance*; and as each new fragment is added, it becomes the vehicle or channel through which the energy of the Holy Ghost passes to incorporate still more.

His Revealing Function

The one aim of the Blessed Spirit is to glorify the Saviour, as the aim of the Saviour was to glorify the Father. The very expressions that were applicable in this connection to the Lord are equally so to the Spirit. Compare, for instance, these two remarkable sentences: 'I have not spoken from myself', and 'He shall not speak from himself'.

If we may so speak, the Holy Spirit shrinks from drawing attention to himself. He is gladdest when all the light that he can focus shines full on the face of Jesus, and men are taken up with him. All that detracts from the pre-eminence of Christ in the heart-life and thought-life of his people is an immense grief to him whose mission is to glorify him by taking of the things that are his, and revealing them to those who love. The life which is most pervaded by the Spirit of Jesus will have most of the beauty of his character reflected in it. And the spirit which is really Spirit-filled will talk more of the Lord Jesus than of the Gracious Agent, whose joy is to reveal him, and to be himself unseen.

Our individual *paracletism* through these priceless functions will be in proportion as we learn the meaning of Galatians 3:14: 'That we might receive the promise of the Spirit by *faith*'. Not by long vigils, nor by prolonged fastings and prayers, nor with a storm of emotion, and the witness of sense, but calmly, quietly, and through faith we may receive all God intends in any of these directions; not once or twice, but repeatedly; not spasmodically, but continuously; not emotionally, but by the adjusted attitude of the consecrated will.

Chapter 9

Escape From the World's Corruption

2 Peter

In no sparing terms, the sacred writers refer to the world of their time. And to this rule the Epistles of Peter are no exception. There is no kind of excess with which he does not charge it. The words lasciviousness, lust and excess of riot, come with sad monotony from his lips. Indeed, the conception of the Second Epistle likens it to Sodom, on which the lawless deeds of the wicked brought the swift judgment of God.

But with equal clearness he defines the position of those whom he addressed, and who had obtained a like precious faith with himself. If the world of their time were another Sodom, they at least were as righteous Lot, distressed with the lascivious life of the wicked, whom the Lord delivered. Would that he had realised and maintained the life to which the Almighty God called him! Then he had enjoyed the free, glad life of the uplands, where Abraham walked with God!

Having escaped! (2 Peter 1:4). How positive this assertion! There at the foot of the cliffs the waves of ink welter, and yonder the bark is slowly going to pieces, but the crew have escaped safe to shore, and, climbing the rocky ledges, are standing far beyond the angry whirl of the waves, and the furthest cast of the spray. Not more absolutely does the Apostle John speak of those who have gotten the victory over the beast, than does this Apostle describe the escape from the corruption of the world, of those who were likely to survive him, and to whom he entrusted words that might help them when he had gone. They stood in the light, where darkness could not include them in its sable empire: they breathed air, in which the germs of contagion could not live: they were surrounded as by a cordon of fire, through which temptation could not pass.

Just escaping (2:18 RV). In the case of some, the escape was in process. They had heard the warning cry of the angels, felt the eager pressure of their hastening hands, and had arisen to flee from them that were living in error, steeped in unconsciousness, solaced by the lullaby of a false peace. It is a great spectacle to behold the awakening of a soul to love, or thought, or some noble conception of the possibilities of life, but it is a greater one to watch it just escaping, passing the city-gates in the early dawn, as the sun is rising on the earth, or beginning to climb the mountain slopes to the shelter of the cave.

After they have escaped the defilements of the world... again entangled therein and overcome (2:20). This is a sad possibility that must ever be borne in mind. We are never saved in this world beyond the fear of relapse. Lot escaped Sodom's doom, but he was entangled again in her sins, and contracted eternal infamy. Many have emerged from the black waves, stood for a little on the cliffs of chrysolite, where the morning light ever shines, but have been sucked back into the remorseless waters. Let him that thinketh he standeth take heed lest he fall. Life is full of perils, and not least so for those who vaunt their deliverance. Our salvation depends on our perpetual reception of the life and grace of the Lord Jesus, and if there is any intermission here, there will be inevitable decrepitude and failure everywhere, and the tempter will easily break into the citadel of the soul.

The method of escape is alluded to in the same phrase. It must be through the knowledge of him that hath called us. We must not be idle or unfruitful in the knowledge of our Lord Jesus Christ; we can only escape the defilements of the world through the knowledge of our Lord and Saviour Jesus

Christ; we must grow in the grace and knowledge of our Lord and Saviour Jesus Christ (1:3, 8; 2:20; 3:18).

To know the second Man, who has undone the havoc of the first; to know him as Jesus, tempted in all points like as we are, though without sin; to know him as Christ, the Anointed of the Father; to know him as Lord, the enthroned King of the heart - these are the conditions on which to know him as Saviour, through whose grace the soul may be delivered from the evil of sin, and know the way of righteousness.

Well may we exclaim with Peter's beloved brother Paul, *that I may know Him*! The believing, adoring, experimental knowledge of what Jesus is and has done, is the entire secret of escaping from the world's corruption, and entering the life in which we may be addressed, as in these Epistles, 'elect sojourners', 'pilgrims and strangers'.

(1) WE KNOW THE LORD JESUS IN HIS SINLESSNESS (1 Peter 2:22).

He took our nature, not as it was in unfallen Adam, but further down the stream, as it was in the seed of Abraham, though he was without the slightest taint of sin. He could face the strictest scrutiny, and cry, 'Which of you convinceth Me of sin?' Herod, Pilate, Judas, searched his character in vain for what would have justified to their conscience their foul and treacherous deeds. 'This Man hath done nothing amiss', was the perpetual verdict of men on the Man Christ Jesus.

But this spotless sinlessness did not diminish the perfect symmetry of his character. He was every whit a Man. All the ages since his death have paid homage to the incomparable beauty of his nature, and extolled him as their example. Pilate's cry has rung down the corridor of the centuries, caught up by a myriad lips, 'Behold the Man'! From which we infer that sin is not indispensable to our nature - it is abnormal, not normal; accidental, not necessary; a disease, a parasite, a blight, but not a constituent part.

Undoubtedly sin is coextensive with the range of human life. Wherever we find man, we encounter the same sins - lying, thieving, adultery, covetousness, murder. These vices, like weeds, are indigenous to every soul, and flourish under every sky. But the fact that one perfect Life has been lived without them, and that those who live nearest it share that emancipation, proves beyond doubt that sin is no necessary part of our nature, but that a time may come when we shall cast it aside, as the ailing child the measles, smallpox, whooping-cough, and other disease, incidental to childhood.

It is a great matter for us to realise what was God's original ideal, when he created us; because all that is foreign to his original purpose must awake his undying opposition. In our combat with it, we may count on his ready and efficient aid.

(2) WE KNOW THE LORD JESUS HAS SUFFERED IN THE FLESH (1 Peter 3:18; 4:1). He suffered for us, and bare our sins in his own body on the tree. He once

offered there a full, perfect and sufficient sacrifice, oblation and satisfaction for the whole world. But he did
more. He died unto sin. He ceased out
of the Time-world, in which sin
reigned. In him, the likeness of our
sinful flesh was nailed up to the igno-
miny and shame of the cross, beneath
the curse of God. And all was done to
emancipate us from the dominion of
sin, so that we should no longer live
the rest of our time to the lust of men,
but to the will of God.

We must understand this aspect of
the death of Christ, if we would secure
all the help the cross was intended to
give. It is not enough to think of Christ
as our Substitute and Sin-bearer; we
must regard him as the Noah, with
whom, in the purpose of God, we
crossed the waters of judgment be-

tween the old world with its curse, and the new world on which the smile of the Creator lay in benediction - the world of resurrection - the new heavens and the new earth, arched by the bow of hope.

'Arm yourselves with the same mind' (or thought, RV margin). Let this thought be deeply inwrought by the power of the Holy Ghost. Let it be the ruling conception of your soul. Muse on it as steadfastly as the saint is said to have considered the *stigmata*. Gird it about you each morning, as the soldier his cuirass before he enters on the fight. Whenever the world approaches with its soft caress, or the flesh allures, or the devil tempts, answer each unhallowed suggestion with the words, 'I cannot do that now; I have passed into a new world, where such things are not admissible; I am seated in Christ Jesus, where all that is unclean and defiling is far down under my feet'. Then reckon on the blessed Spirit to make your boasting good, and to realise in you all that Jesus accomplished when he breathed out his Spirit in the last throes of death. There is no need to be overcome of sin. We are risen: we have ascended; we are one with Jesus in his glorious triumph. The Spirit that raised Jesus from the dead dwells in us, and is prepared to realise in us, as in miniature, all that glory and victory which he wrought in our glorious Lord. 'He that hath suffered in the flesh (and we have done that in Jesus) hath ceased from sin.' Let us ponder these deep and precious words.

(3) WE KNOW THAT THE LORD JESUS HAS PURCHASED US FOR HIMSELF.

This thought is a favourite one with the Apostle Peter: 'Redeemed, not with silver and gold, but with precious blood'. 'A people for God's own possession.' 'Denying even the Master that bought them.'

In the wide market-place of the world, we stood for sale; nay, rather had become sold in sin, and enslaved to the will of the Prince of the Power of the air. But Jesus bought us for himself. We are his, not only by the gift of the Father, but by the purchase of his most precious blood.

Consecration is simply the restoring to Christ his own property; recognising and answering his rightful claims; saying gladly and reverently, 'I am thine, O Lord'. When once this attitude has been thoughtfully assumed, it answers all the questions which arise in the conduct of life. These hands are my Master's, they may not touch the unclean thing; these feet are his, they may not go in forbidden paths; these senses and faculties are his, they must not be used outside the circle of his will; this body is his, no voice but his can control or direct it; these members are his, they may not be presented as weapons of unrighteousness unto sin. Reasonings like these make us feel that we dare not sin. A holy fear forbids that we shall grieve our Master, or injure his reputation in the world. 'We cannot do this wickedness,' we cry, 'for we are not our own; we have been bought with a price, and we must glorify our Master in our body and spirit, which are his.' And as we say the words in the energy of the Holy Ghost, lo! the snare is broken, and we are escaped.

(4) WE KNOW THAT THROUGH OUR LORD JESUS CHRIST WE HAVE BECOME PARTAKERS OF THE DIVINE NATURE (2 Peter 1:4).

There is no more potent wedge than this text to split the modern error that all men are equally the children of God. There is a lower sense (that in which the Apostle Paul used the words on Mars Hill) in which all men are the children of God, since they have sprung from his creative hand, but this is not the meaning in which the apostles used the words when they said, 'Because ye are sons, he hath sent forth the Spirit of his Son in our hearts', and 'Now are we the sons of God, and it doth not yet appear what we shall be'.

Man may be the offspring of God, but he is not the son of God until he has, in regeneration, received the very life of God into his nature. The Spirit of God begets in the believing and receptive spirit that very life which was in the Father before the worlds were made, and was manifested in the Lord Jesus. Thus we become partakers of the Divine nature. As a child partakes of its mother's life, so do we partake of God's. We love what he loves, hate as he hates, and make his purposes our own. There is, moreover, a perpetual communication and interchange of life, as of water between the ocean and the inlets into the land. As the tide rises in the one, it rises in the other; and the movements of the one are transmitted to the other.

This is the secret of escaping from the defilement around. We have become possessed of a new set of shuttles which are ever weaving desires for purity and righteousness, and in contrast to these, we have no desire for the old sins. Nay, more: Christ is within us, and is eager to reproduce himself in us, and as he does so, we are weaned from the things of which we are now ashamed, and hunger with an insatiable desire to be partakers of the holiness of God.

This is even better than an escape - that Jesus lives in us by his Spirit, and seeks to manifest through our yielded lives his own glorious character.

Chapter 10

Other Worldliness

'By honour and dishonour, by evil report and good report: as deceivers, and yet true; As unknown, and yet well known; as dying, and, behold, we live; as chastened, and not killed; As sorrowful, yet always rejoicing; as poor, yet making many rich; as having nothing, and yet possessing all things'
(2 Corinthians 6:8-10).

By the operation of that mysterious force which matter exerts on matter, the formula of which is contained in Newton's definition of the law of gravitation, we are all kept close to the surface of our earth. However swift its motion, there is no fear of our being flung up from the solid ground into the air, and away into space. But we do not equally realise that, to a certain extent, the sun also, millions of miles distant, constantly exercises an attractive force, by virtue of which we are being insensibly drawn towards it.

We are incessantly subject to the operation of two mighty forces. On the one hand, attracted downwards to the earth, on the other, upwards to the sun. But we are unconscious of the latter, because the mass of our planet is so much nearer. Suppose, however, that we could begin to rise from the surface of our earth by the exercise of our will, and in the track of the Ascension of our Lord, every mile that we left it, the earth would attract us less, and the sun more. When, however, we had traversed some considerable distance across the abyss between our native home and the source of light, we should come to a point where the attraction of the earth would be exactly balanced by that of the sun, and we should remain in perfect equipoise, balanced between the drawing power of the earth on the one side, and of the sun on the other. But when we had passed a hair's breadth beyond that point, we should be caught into a swifter current of mystic power, and begin, with ever-increasing velocity, to rush towards the glowing surface of the sun.

This illustration will help us to understand our relation to two worlds. By our natural birth, we are closely related to the time-sphere, the system of things around us, with all its alternations of experience, its heat and cold, its light and shade, its joy and sorrow. We cannot dissociate ourselves from the century, the city, the circle, to which we belong. But by our second birth we become related to the unseen and eternal, to the world that gathers around the New Jerusalem as its metropolis, and finds its centre in the person of our Lord.

In the earlier part of our Christian life, we are deeply and perpetually conscious of the conflicting forces that contend for us. On the one side, habits, companions, associations strive strongly to keep their hold on us, whilst Heaven begins steadily to pull us away. Presently we reach the point of equilibrium and equipoise. Time and eternity, the worlds seen and unseen, exert an equal power; we hover between the two; now dipping back into the one, now borne swiftly towards the other. But the more blessed experience is yet to come, wherein we are hardly aware of the pull of earth, because we are abandoned to the strong and blessed current which is bearing us nearer to our true centre of bliss in God.

Holy souls have ever felt the momentum and energy of that current. It was this which drew Abraham from Charran, and made the patriarchs willing to dwell in tents. And it is this which has made the saints pass through the earth, as Christian and Faithful through Vanity Fair, regardless of the enticement that would arrest their steps. 'Our citizenship is in heaven, from whence also we wait for a Saviour.' 'We look for and hasten unto the coming of the day of God.'

Other worldliness is the true method of unworldliness. The lives of many amongst us are full of negations, with very little of the positive and affirmative. It is as though we were to take one side of the Apostle's paradoxes, without the other. Unknown, but not well-known; dying, but not living; sorrowful, but never rejoicing; poor, yet never enriched; as having nothing in this world, and possessing nothing in the next. Miserable indeed is such a life as this. It is as if we were to try to wrench ourselves from the earth-sphere by the force of our will, before ever we had felt or yielded to the beckoning attraction of the sun.

The easier and better way is to surrender ourselves more entirely and obediently to the tender constraint of heaven. Think less of the world you are leaving than of that which is attracting you. Seek to be heavenly-minded by the grace and power of the Holy Spirit. Lay up treasures in heaven by the judicious administration of all your possessions on earth. Set your affections on things above, not on things on the earth. Let the drift and set of your thoughts be towards the movements of the blessed Lord as he goes forth, followed by the armies of heaven, to put down all rule and authority and power. Tread the streets of the heavenly city, lave in its fountain, pluck the fruits from its tree of life, hold converse with its inhabitants. 'Ye are come unto mount Zion, unto the city of the living God, the heavenly Jerusalem, and the spirits of just men made perfect.'

Then almost insensibly you will

become unworldly. You will view without heartbreak the wreck of patterns of things in the heavens, because you have found the heavenly things themselves. You will not scruple to part with all your sham jewels, because you have found the pearl of great price. You will not view with much chagrin the fading of the chaplet of earthly glory, because you have become possessed of the incorruptible crown that fadeth not away.

Let us reverse the Apostle's magnificent series of paradoxes. Let us be true, transparent, and sincere before the eye of God and his holy angels, and we shall not be greatly moved, though all men count us deceivers. Let us seek to be well-known in heaven as those that pray and work for the coming of the kingdom, and we shall be content to live as unknown in the esteem of this babbling and vain world. Let us be quick with God's life beating high within us, and we shall be willing to fall into the ground to die. Let us drink deep from the chalices of heaven's gladness, and we shall bear the stings of whips of time with patient composure. Let us amass the treasures of a noble character, and possess ourselves of the unsearchable riches of Christ, and we shall be content to be poor, and to have nothing. Give us heaven, O God, and we shall be weaned from the breasts of consolation that are everything to others. Inevitably, a life like this will bring us into collision with men around us. It could not be otherwise. They are being swept along by the earth-current, we are on the heaven-current.

They are being drawn downward, we upward; so there must be antagonism and collision as we pass. 'Marvel not if the world hate you. If ye were of the world, the world would love its own; but because ye are not of the world, but I have chosen you out of the world, therefore the world hateth you.'

We may gauge the directness and swiftness of our course heavenward by remarking the intensity of the world's hatred and scorn; yet we must never cease to pity it and weep for it, and exert ourselves to the uttermost to deliver those who are being swept to ruin by its insidious streams. 'He was in the world, and the world was made by him, and the world knew him not.' But he *so* loved the world. Otherworldliness weans us from that love of the world, which is unholy and harmful; and inspires a love which is pure and holy, self-sacrificing and divine.

The world is the inspired symbol of transience. It passeth away like the shows of a theatre. Permanent though it appear, the scene is changing whilst we gaze, like a dissolving view. And even before it fades, its lust is gone (1 John 2:17). The power to enjoy dies down in satiety. Woeful indeed would it be if some day we were to wake up to find the thirst of desire burning within the soul, whilst the zest of enjoyment and the source of satisfaction were gone for ever! Is not this the worm that never dies, the fire that is never quenched?

But thrice blessed is it to obey the divine summons, and to yield to the attraction of the Unseen and Eternal. Because the power of pure enjoyment is ever on the increase, and the taste becomes more refined to detect the flavour of the best wine, kept to the last, and there is always some sweeter note, some more delicate hue of colour, some more rapturous experience of bliss. Though we penetrate into the divine nature for countless ages, there will always be something in God we have never explored, and always increased power to appreciate and enjoy. Let us begin to yield ourselves more than ever to the attractions and blessedness of that great Voice from heaven, which calls us to come up thither. Leaving what is behind, let us walk - let us run - let us mount up with wings as eagles.

Chapter 11

'The Pitcher and God's Well'

*'Search the scriptures; for in them
ye think ye have eternal life: and
they are they which testify of me'
(John 5:39).*

In the rush of the present day there has
been a great multiplication of Daily
Text-Books, and the fear is lest many
may get into the habit of supposing
that they have done their duty by their
Bibles when they have caught up a
text, or glanced down a page of carefully prepared text mosaic. But one
might as well suppose that it were
possible to sustain physical health by
eating all one's meals at restaurant

bars, selecting a choice dainty here or a biscuit there. Certainly the daily text is better than nothing, but it is a very poor substitute for deliberate, careful study of the Word of God.

The whole Bible bears evidence of the care with which each generation fed on the Scriptures antecedent to itself. The Psalter bears witness to the value David set on the limited sacred library he possessed, for his Psalms are strongly tinctured and coloured by its thoughts and phrases. Micah reappears in Isaiah, and Daniel in the Apocalypse. The Old Testament is the perpetual standard of appeal to the writers of the New, and where they do not actually quote it, it is not difficult to discover evidences of its influence on their modes of thought and expression. The Old Testament is the quarry of the New. It is no exaggeration to say that the aim of the New Testament is the unfolding and explanation of the treasures of the Old. When, therefore, we turn to our Bibles, let us remember the hands by which those precious pages have been turned, the eyes by which each expression has been scanned, and the hearts which have been taught and nourished by those sacred words. In the case of the Old Testament this vast host would of course comprise all the writers of the New, and best of all, the Son of Man himself; in the case of the New, the entire Church of the redeemed. Let us read as an Augustine might have done, when the voice in the gardens of Tagaste whispered, *Tolle, lege*; or as Luther might have done, in the Augustinian convent; or as Livingstone might have done, from his worn Testament, in the heart of Africa. New though the page of your Bible may appear, fresh from the press, it is soiled by the use and wet with the tears of all the generations.

Read deliberately - In order to keep the peace with their consciences, some read standing bolt upright in their rooms, in momentary expectation of the breakfast-bell; others glance down their portion when wearied out with the day's toil and about to sleep. Where this is unavoidable, it would be unreasonable to complain, and without doubt, the miracle of the manna is repeated, by which, it is said, 'they who gathered little had no lack'.

But for perhaps the majority of those who read this paper there is leisure to eat; and it is with the view of helping them that these words are penned. Take time, or make time. If you have to curtail your Bible-reading or your prayer, let it be the latter; for it is less important for you to speak to God than to hear what God has to say to you. Sit quietly down in your most comfortable chair, prepared to have a good time. It seems to me a mistake to read the Bible in a kneeling or constrained position, whilst you read your favourite author ensconced in comfort. Enter into your closet, and shut your door; give time for the world's glare to pass from your eyes, and its tumult from your ears. Imitate the listener at the telephone, who shuts himself in the little cupboard, and sets himself down to talk with his unseen friend.

Read consecutively - Nothing is

more irreverent to the spirit of Scripture than to read a passage here or there as the Book falls open. By all means read the Bible through. Adopt one of the many plans now in vogue. Whatever it be, mind to read the New Testament along with the Old, and perhaps spending longer over its deeper doctrinal portions than over its narratives.

Use the references - It is of great importance to use a Bible with good marginal references. I owe more than I can tell to the habit of turning to the parallel passages, first, as suggested by the *Annotated Paragraph Bible*, and lately by the *Treasury of Scripture Knowledge* published by Bagster. The latter is specially valuable now that I use habitually the Revised Version, which, of course, is destitute of the marginal references of the editions of the Authorised Version. There is so much to be said in favour of the use of the Revised Version, its freshness, accuracy, suggestive marginal notes, paragraphing, and absence of misleading headings to chapters and pages, that it is a great loss to have to supply the marginal references from elsewhere.

But this lack may be amply met by the latter of the books mentioned above. After reading your portion carefully and thoughtfully through, open your *Treasury* and go through it again, turning to the passages indicated, and you will find almost invariably that fresh light will come to the passage already read, as flints struck together emit sparks, and that some direct message is furnished to the soul by a passage in another part of Scripture.

It is, of course, competent to pursue the references of an ordinary Bible without the use of the special books named; and in time it may be well to discard all such references, and to make your own. Some of the most valuable sidelights to Scripture occur to oneself after a course of years devoted to this careful comparison of scripture with scripture. At the same time, we should be reverently careful not to connect passages on account of their verbal or fanciful connections. This habit is disastrous, and diverts the mind from the intelligent study and appreciation of Scripture. There are so many obvious and necessary quotations and references that it is needless and wrong to import the fantastical and extravagant.

Study books as a whole - Permit me, though at the risk of being counted egotistical, to tell a favourite practice. I like, especially when I am on a long journey, or during my vacation, to take an Epistle or Gospel or Prophecy, and read it over and over. Take, for instance, the First Epistle of John. You read it the first day without any special light striking you. You receive the general impression that it is about love, and that is all. You read it the second day, and the third, and these impressions are confirmed, but, in addition, you become aware that certain words are constantly recurring, which seem like stepping-stones across a brook. After some more readings, these appear as the nuclei of the treatise; and probably you will underline them, each with its own colour or mark, to show their relation. In this way the object of the book is clearly defined, and the details fall into place. It is like getting a plan of the country before beginning to traverse it.

What new interest attaches to Bible study, when we discover the secret of each book, in this way, for ourselves! To have been told it by another will never be of the same value as to find it for ourselves. In this sense it is true that to those who overcome their lethargy and natural indolence, a white stone is given, and in the stone a new name, which only he who receives it knows. Be sure of this, that every book has its message, and that all its hard and difficult, rugged or stony bits, its seeming contradictions to the rest of Scripture, will yield when the drift of the whole is apprehended. We must interpret the parts by the purpose of the whole.

Read the Bible topically - There are some who take a word and study it throughout the Bible, but it is difficult to do this unless you are sure that the original word is always rendered by the same words in the English version, otherwise you will get into endless confusion. Take the word *perfect*, for instance, which stands for three or four Greek words, one or two of which have nothing to do with moral purity and beauty. If you wish to study words, you must use a Hebrew or Greek Concordance, or its equivalent in English; then it is extremely interesting and instructive to trace the development of the meaning, the increased connotation of a word, like Faith, or Love, or Repentance.

It is, however, even better to take a subject and trace it through the Bible. Nothing so convinces one of the homogeneity of the Bible as this. Though written by so many different authors, over so great a lapse of time, it is essentially one Book, the product of one informing mind, the Word of God.

Take, for instance, the overthrow of Satan, as shadowed forth in the opening chapters. There are constant references made to the progress of the great fight, until we reach the casting of the devil into the great pit of the Apocalypse, and these are the staples of the chain. The links are found in nearly every page, which tells of the perpetual feud between the seed of the woman and the seed of the serpent, between the armies that follow the Lamb on white horses and the principalities and powers of darkness.

Traces of it appear in Psalm 91, with its references to lion and dragon; in Luke 10, with our Lord's assurance that his disciples should tread on all the power of the enemy; and in Ephesians 1 and 6, where allusion is made to Christ's triumphant ascension above all the dark powers. What a flood of light such a study casts on the whole course of Revelation!

Read the Bible with pen in hand - Mark the words that call to one another in the same chapter, draw lines of connection between parallel phrases, insert your own references, underscore your favourite texts, put date or names against verses which have a history attached to them. And when one Bible is worn out, be careful not to transfer your markings to an-

other, lest your views become stere-
otyped, and you always read your
Bible under the same aspect. But
begin to make another set of references and markings. Thus we should
wear our Bibles out at least as often as
we change our skins. Small pens making but a faint mark are provided for
this purpose.

Read the Bible devotionally - It is a
bush in which the Divine fire is burning, take the shoes from off your feet.
It is a shrine where the Ark of God is
resting, draw near with reverence.
There is a great danger lest we should
multiply maps, and commentaries, and
illustrative books of oriental travel, to
the loss of the devotional attitude. We
should approach the Bible, as Jesus
must have done in those thirty years of
meditation and seclusion. Let not those

meddle with criticism who have not time to give themselves to the study of the whole question. Our best practical proof that the Bible is inspired is by its effect on us in our highest moods. Let us look to it for the stimulus and culture of our best life. This makes it the god of Books to us. And let us open it with the ancient prayer, 'Open thou mine eyes, that I may behold wondrous things out of thy law'.

Let me urge on my readers the repeated reading of the longest Psalm, 119. It is of inestimable benefit in inculcating that frame of mind which is necessary when we enter the threshold of this ancient fane, whose walls were built by reverent hands long cold, whose windows admit the light of eternity, whose storied heights ring ever with the notes of the Divine voice. Of that Psalm, the perpetual refrain is, as it should be of our life, *Teach me thy statutes*.

Read the Bible practically - Whatever you read, turn forthwith to practice. We have only as much truth as we do. It is not the hearer, but the doer, who is blessed. It is one of the catchwords of Deuteronomy, 'Hearken and Do'. Only as we hear the words of Christ, and do them, shall we be like a house founded on a rock that shall stand immovable against the burst of the storm.

I have often noticed people in a convention taking down every word most diligently, and at the close saying complacently, 'I have got it all here'. What have they got? Only the signs, the counters, the embodiment of truth; but not the truth itself. That is theirs only so far as they live up to what they have heard. And it is better to do one thing for God because he has bidden us, than to cram a hundred into our minds as though for a competitive examination.

Each day read your chapter or passage with the idea that you are receiving your marching-orders, that there is some new service to render, some new duty to perform, some new virtue to acquire. Let the attitude of your soul be indicated by Samuel's word, 'Speak, Lord, for thy servant heareth'. When you hear, do. What you have been taught, embody in action. Take the precepts of the Bible as requiring literal and immediate obedience. Let the Spirit *guide* you into all truth; the onward and upward stepping of obedience, beneath his leading, will be

the best commentary on what is difficult and obscure. So shall you climb
to the Pisgah height, where all the
realms of Bible truth to the utmost sea
shall lie apparent to your gaze.

Other large print titles available
from
Christian Focus Publications

Assurance
J C Ryle
ISBN 1 871 676 053   160 pages

Comfort In Sorrow
Robert Murray McCheyne
ISBN 1 85792 0120   160 pages

Gems From Genesis
Barbara Honour
ISBN 0 906731 33 X   128 pages

God Always Care
C. H. Spurgeon
ISBN 1 871 676 398   96 pages

God Can Be Trusted
George Muller
ISBN 1 871676 55 X   80 pages

Heaven
J C Ryle
ISBN 1 871 676 754   96 pages

Longing For Heaven
Horatius Bonar
ISBN 1 85792 0112   60 pages

Peace, Perfect Peace
F. B. Meyer
ISBN 1 871 676 401   96 pages

Songs of the Heart
A selection of well known hymns
ISBN 1 871 676 606   96 pages

Starlight Through The Shadows
Frances Ridley Havergal
ISBN 1 871 676 568   96 pages

Twelve Baskets Full
ISBN 1 857 920 082   384 pages
A daily reading book for the
whole year, with each month's
readings provided by a different
well known Christian, and ed-
ited by Elizabeth Catherwood.
Contributors include Rebecca
Manley-Pippert, R T Kendall
and Philip Hacking.